GLASGOW'S TRAMS

The Twilight Years

By
Paul Anderson
and W.A.C. Smith

IRWELL
PRESS

Copyright Irwell Press,
Paul Anderson and W.A.C. Smith
ISBN 1-871608-53-8

ACKNOWLEDGEMENTS

The authors are indebted to Juliet Whitworth of Barrow upon
Soar for the line drawings and Tim Shuttleworth of Ludlow for
printing the photographs. W.A.C. Smith wishes particularly to
thank Doris for her help, encouragement, patience and
painstaking proof reading in Glasgow, and this is echoed by
Paul Anderson in Leicester.

Six new cars, Nos.1393-1398, emerged from Coplawhill Works in 1954 and were destined to be the last trams built for the Glasgow fleet. They were of Coronation design, but were slightly modified and had bogies and motors from Liverpool cars destroyed in the recent Green Lane Depot fire. At the north end of Eglinton Street on 3rd June 1960, No.1395 approaches Bridge Street on service 3 from Mosspark to Park Road. Bridge Street Underground station on the left survives in rebuilt form, the tenements having been demolished. The Coliseum Cinema, identified by the tower above the tram, is now a bingo hall.

First Published
in the United Kingdom by
IRWELL PRESS 1998
59A, High Street,
Clophill,
Bedfordshire MK45 4BE
Printed and Bound by
DPI Printers, Luton, England

CONTENTS

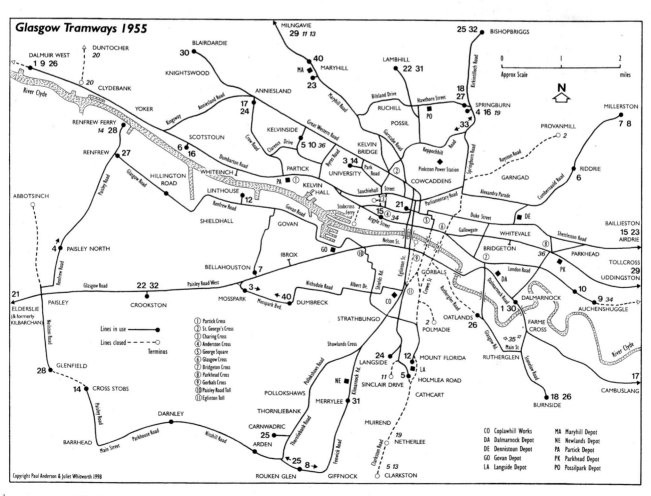

Glasgow Tramways 1955

An evocative view of Argyle Street in the heart of Glasgow on 11th March 1961. Seen from the top deck of a westbound 'caur', Kilmarnock Bogie No.1133 heads east on service 26 from Scotstoun to Farme Cross, near Rutherglen. The last tram procession passed this way in torrential rain on 4th September 1962. Marks & Spencer's store has long been completed and shoppers continue to flock along Argyle Street, but fortunately cars and buses have been excluded. Modern trams are the most civilised form of urban transport and would even be in harmony with this busy pedestrianised area.

RECOLLECTIONS by W.A.C. Smith

Although born in Glasgow, my early years were spent in Aberdeen which had a small but efficient tramway system. At that time all of its cars were four-wheelers, some still with open balconies, so a family visit to Glasgow for the 1938 Empire Exhibition was a revelation, with journeys on the superb new Coronation cars. Even today, sixty years on, the Coronations are considered by some to have been unsurpassed as short stage public service vehicles.

Soon after the outbreak of war we moved back to Glasgow, taking up residence in the west end of the city where we were to be on the periphery of the Clydebank Blitz. The night of Thursday 13th March 1941 was of almost unbelievable clarity with a full moon when, at 9pm, the air raid sirens gave their eerie warning. It soon became obvious that

this was no minor attack, as the unrelenting drone of enemy aircraft mingled with the crash of exploding bombs, and an almost continuous barrage of anti-aircraft fire continued until around 5.30am.

Some two hours into the raid three parachute land mines fell in close proximity to our flat, blowing out windows and doors and covering my schoolwork on the kitchen table with a thick layer of soot. In the early hours, ignoring parental remonstrations, I slipped out for a quick look round and found the streets littered with spent incendiary bombs and other debris. A shoemaker's wooden hut between the Queen Street and Central Low Level railway lines was blazing furiously. A more chilling sight was a sinister pall of smoke, dust and choking fumes hanging over a block of flats which had suffered a direct hit - many years later I discovered that survivors trapped in the rubble had died because of the inefficiency of the rescue services.

A dozen or more trams, all Standards I recall, were stranded in Clarence Drive without power, their crews sheltering as best they could. Although I was not aware

George Square, overlooked by the magnificent City Chambers since 1888, has been an obvious venue for celebrations and festivities in the centre of Glasgow over the past two centuries. It was here that trams had to nudge through ecstatic crowds on VE Day, for instance. In more placid circumstances, Standard No.41 on service 1 from Scotstoun West to Springfield Road and Coronation No.1206 on route 23 from Maryhill to Baillieston negotiate the north side of George Square on 13th February 1960. The North British Hotel in the background, now renamed the Copthorne, still fronts Queen Street station.

The Kilpatrick Hills form a tranquil background to this scene at Dalmuir on 23rd November 1955, but the ruined building on the right is a stark reminder of the Clydebank Blitz of 1941. Kilmarnock Bogie No.1092 and Standard No.183 stand at the Dalmuir West terminus of route 9 which formed the backbone of the Glasgow system. No.1092 was about to set off for Auchenshuggle in the East End via Dumbarton Road, Argyle Street and London Road.

of it at the time, car No.6 had already been destroyed in Nelson Street on the south side of the river with considerable loss of life. A second raid, somewhat less prolonged, took place the following night and tram services were not fully restored for several weeks. One memory of the aftermath of these raids is the temporary replacement of broken windows in trams by opaque glass, presumably all that was immediately available.

This was the sharp end of war, but for most of the civilian population of Glasgow the years of conflict were a dreary succession of increasing restrictions and decreasing services. In summer 1943 there was an extensive reorganisation of tram operations, with longer routes cut to minimise delays caused by the ever increasing number of breakdowns. Furthermore, tram stops in busy city centre streets were split and provided with 'Q' signs. *The Glasgow Herald* noted that on the first day *'all tramcars drew up with the rear platform directly opposite the appropriate stopping place and the queues were shepherded forwarded by tramway officials ...there was not the wild rush that characterised Union Street until last week'*. Thus was born the now familiar queue. A limited number of night services ran, but priority was given to workers with passes, which occasionally led to scuffles at the boarding points in St. Vincent Street.

Derailments and breakdowns were commonplace, and on 9th August 1944 there was a major failure at Pinkston Power Station which resulted in mounted police having to disperse crowds seeking transport in Argyle Street. Fares rose again (to a maximum of four pence!) although members of the armed forces were allowed to travel any distance for one penny. Most conductors and some drivers were female because of the scarcity of manpower, and during the rush hour trams carried auxiliary conductors because of the crush of passengers. From 17th September 1944 the black-out was replaced by a dim-out, this being lifted on 23rd April 1945 when shades and blue paint were speedily removed from tram interior lighting, making life much easier for crew and passengers alike.

I had an aunt who was much given to a 'hurl' on a tram during the war. With longer distance travel actively discouraged, lengthy queues at cinemas and little to buy in the shops, this made sense. By accompanying her I soon gained a good working knowledge of the system which, at its Golden Jubilee on 1st July 1944, boasted 135 route miles worked by 1,207 cars, according to official figures. By now, my interest in railways was such that I was keeping detailed notes (as I still do) but I did not record tramway journeys to the same extent. However, I have

unearthed a log of a journey, no doubt inspired by Cecil J. Allen's *British Locomotive Practice and Performance* in *The Railway Magazine*, which is of some curiosity value. This is a summary:

Journey: Glasgow Corporation Tramways Service 5 Kelvinside to Clarkston; Tram: Coronation No.1214; Date: Monday 19th April 1945. Kelvinside - 8.29pm; Charing Cross - 8.39pm; Renfield Street - 8.45pm; Eglinton Toll - 8.56pm; Cathcart - 9.08pm; Clarkston - 9.19pm. Total journey time: 50 minutes for 9½ miles. Return was by Standard tram No.481, the journey taking 47 minutes. The current running time for Greater Glasgow buses on the equivalent service is 53 minutes!

VE Day, Tuesday 8th May 1945, brought vast crowds to the city centre. Even with police travelling on the front platform, trams were literally having to force their way through the singing and dancing throng in George Square. Despite the return to normality, a considerable backlog of maintenance remained and on 11th August 1945 I was travelling on Kilmarnock Bogie No.1118, eastbound along Dumbarton Road on service 9, when an axle fractured as we passed through Clydebank. It was decided to continue in an attempt to reach Partick Depot and we set off at a noisy snail's pace.

At Yoker, by which time at least a dozen cars were trailing us, there was further discussion and eventually the following trams set back over the crossover in batches and ran wrong line to Scotstoun. This caused consternation amongst motorists who were confronted by trams approaching at speed on the wrong side of the road!

Figures released by the Transport Department in 1946 revealed that of a total of 11,500 employees in 1939, more than 3,000 went into the armed forces or essential war work. Also, the number of passenger journeys by tram had risen from 457 million in 1939 to 572 million in 1945 - astonishing, considering the population of Glasgow and its satellite towns served by the network was less than 1½ million at the time.

However, returning from the army in 1950, I found change afoot. Some were minor, such as advertising on the sides of the trams and an abortive attempt to return to the once familiar route colours which had adorned the upper deck panels before the war. Others were more significant, such as the new Cunarder cars and a couple of extensions to the system. But the long-discussed trolleybus operation was now a reality. Much more ominous was the trickle of abandonments, destined to become a flood. This prompted me to add tram photography to my railway and shipping interests, the results of which figure in the following pages.

Above. There was plenty of scope for a 'hurl' on a Glasgow tram during the early 1950s, as there were nearly thirty main services and some of them ventured far from the city centre. One of the longest routes was 14 from University to Cross Stobs at Barrhead and this involved some decidedly rural running as a bonus. On 29th September 1956, Standard No.824 had just left Nitshill Road at Darnley and is climbing across open country on ballasted private track. That very week, however, a notice had appeared in the cars stating 'On and after 30th September, the service between Arden and Cross Stobs will not be operated.'

Below. Recollections by Paul Anderson. My father took me to Glasgow for a short holiday during August 1962. In those days, there was the luxury of the 'Thames - Clyde Express' through from Leicester to St. Enoch. In the middle of the week, I eagerly stumbled up the stairs of a tram as it paused in semi-darkness where Argyle Street hid beneath the platforms of Central station. Half an hour later, the excitement of the journey out west aboard Cunarder No.1372 was recorded with my box camera at Dalmuir West. We stayed at the YMCA in Bothwell Street and one morning at the breakfast counter I made a juvenile comment about the service being different at the hostel in Earls Court. The response was instant: 'This is Glasgow, not London, sonny.' I have been addicted to the city ever since! Photograph Paul Anderson.

The first 693 Standard cars dating from 1898 to 1910 were built with curved panels below the driver's windows whilst the balance of 312 which appeared between 1910 and 1924 had angular dashes. Representatives of the two styles are seen together at leafy Garrowhill crossover in Baillieston Road on 26th September 1958. 'Hexagonal Dash' No.150 on a service 15 short working waits for 'Round Dash' No.310 from Baillieston to pass. Both cars are heading for Anderston Cross, just west of the city centre.

CHAPTER 2
THE GLASGOW 'CAURS'

Glasgow's trams were the most famous in the world and symbolised the city as much as shipbuilding. A feature which made them so distinctive in pre-war years was the practice of painting the upper deck panels in one of five route colours - green for Knightswood and Airdrie (service 1), white for University and Mosspark (3), red for Dalmuir West and Auchenshuggle (9), yellow for Mount Florida and Paisley Road Roll (12), blue for Milngavie and Renfrew Ferry (4) and so on. The advent of the stylish Coronation cars in 1937, followed by wartime economies, meant the end of route colours - although there was an abortive attempt to revive them in the early 1950s. Even so, the unlikely yet highly satisfactory livery of green,

orange, cream and maroon clearly distinguished Glasgow trams from those elsewhere.

The city's first tramways were built by the Corporation under the Glasgow Street Tramways Act of 1870 and horse car operation was leased to the Glasgow Tramway and Omnibus Company for 23 years. With much

ceremony, this organisation began working the initial route from St. George's Cross to Eglinton Toll on 19th August 1872. No less than twenty sections of track had been opened by 1876 and a further twenty came in 1880-82 and 1886-88. Instead of renewing the lease, Glasgow Corporation decided to work the flourishing 31 mile system itself and an Act was passed to this effect in 1891. But negotiations to purchase premises and vehicles failed, so the newly formed Tramways Department built nine depots and bought 290 cars together with 3,500 horses in time for the start of operations on 1st July 1894. The routes, which extended out as far as Maryhill, Springburn,

By 1924 new fleet numbers were being allocated to cars acquired from the Paisley and Airdrie systems, so the last five Standards had to fit in where slots were available. During the overcast evening of 20th April 1961, No.1051 on service 26 from Scotstoun to Farme Cross unloads at Glasgow Cross. At least four of the passengers were clad in the mandatory gabardine raincoats of the period and were quite probably heading for nearby places of refreshment. The entrance to Glasgow Cross station on the Central Low Level line is behind the tram and the associated smoke vent or 'lung' is identified by the ornate screen embellished with thistles.

When the Paisley District Tramways were acquired in 1923, the 68 cars had 1000 added to their numbers by Glasgow. No.1017 was one of seventeen ex-Paisley vehicles converted to single deck for the Clydebank - Duntocher route which opened in 1924-25 and had to negotiate a low bridge at Kilbowie Road. Six Standards received the same treatment. The Duntocher trams were replaced by buses in 1949 and No.1017 subsequently became a 'School' car for training motormen. It is seen on its own single track in Coplaw Street opposite Coplawmill works on 14th February 1956. The tram, built way back in 1904 by the British Electric Car Company, was finally withdrawn in 1960.

Pollokshaws and Mount Florida, were distinguished by colours from this date.

Following the examination of various tramway systems in England, Europe and the United States, it was decided to adopt electric traction in Glasgow, to replace of the horse drawn vehicles. The first route, from Mitchell Street to Springburn, began working on 13th October 1898 and the new cars were regarded with awe and excitement. Generating equipment was installed at Springburn Depot in Keppochhill Road, but this was replaced by the huge Pinkston Power Station at Port Dundas

After the relentless output of Standards, there was a touch of innovation in the air at Coplawhill by the mid-1920s. No.1089, a single-deck, high-speed, large-capacity bogie vehicle with hints of Pacific Electric in Los Angeles about it, emerged from the Works. It was nicknamed 'Baillie Burtt's car' after the Convenor of the Tramways Committee at the time. Problems arose in service and it was soon confined to the Duntocher route until this closed in 1949. After a period in store, the oddity was sent to Partick Depot for shipyard specials. On 6th June 1960 it is seen heading along Dumbarton Road in Yoker, bound for Clydebank.

The Kilmarnock Bogies, built by outside suppliers in 1927-28, were a determined attempt to provide a powerful high-capacity successor to the Standards, but they were prone to derailments. As a result, they were usually confined to the relatively straight east-west routes. At the end of the evening rush on 14th July 1960, No.1118 turns out of Dumbarton Road into Hayburn Street and heads towards Partick Depot under the watchful eye of the duty inspector. The view was taken from Partickhill station on the Queen Street Low Level line.

on 24th April 1901. Electrification stimulated a massive expansion of the system and by 1907 Glasgow cars could be seen way out of the city at Dalmuir, Uddingston and Giffnock. There was also a fair amount of 'infill' along suburban routes linking the main arteries. The Airdrie & Coatbridge Tramways Company was acquired in 1922, followed by the Paisley District system a year later. Further extensions came during the 1920s and 1930s and the last stretch of new track opened in 1949, by which time some closures had already taken place.

Glasgow's first electric trams were 21 'room and kitchen' single-deck, centre-entrance bogie cars, Nos.665 to 685, and two open-top, single-truck double deckers, Nos.686 and 687. They were built at the Corporation's Coplawhill Works and at first worked the Springburn route. As electrification proceeded, 120 horse cars were

Despite modernisation of the Standards in 1928-30, complaints about the lack of comfort in Glasgow's trams persisted. The response from Coplawhill Works was exceptional. During 1937 a sleek streamlined car appeared on the city streets, the first of 152 Coronations often described as the finest urban passenger transport vehicles ever. They were brought to the attention of the public at large by their use on routes serving the 1938 Empire Exhibition in Bellahouston Park. On 27th May 1961, Coronation No.1223 passes elegant villas in Stonelaw Road, Rutherglen while working service 18 from Burnside to Springburn.

Following the success of the Coronations, Kilmarnock Bogie No.1100 was rebuilt in 1941 with modified electrical equipment, separate driving cabs, platform doors and semi-streamlined ends displaying coloured route indicator lights. Nothing came of the experiment and the car was relegated to shipyard specials from Partick Depot. It is seen leaving its home base on 15th April 1960 bound for Clydebank, to pick up workers from the John Brown Yard.

converted to electric traction and became Nos.1 to 120. The remainder were scrapped despite their modest age. Meanwhile, an intensive programme of new construction got underway. The two double-deckers were very popular with the public, so Nos.686 and 687 proved the first of no less than 1,005 Standard four-wheel cars which became part of the very fabric of Glasgow for nearly sixty years. Apart from eighty supplied by the Gloucester Carriage & Wagon Company, they all emerged from Coplawhill Works.

The first 693 Standards were designated 'Round Dash' because of the shape of their front panels and appeared between 1898 and 1910, an average rate of one every 5½ days! From 1910 to 1924 a further 312 entered service, these being 'Hexagonal Dash' cars. The earlier ones were progressively rebuilt and the whole fleet was modernised in 1928-30. A summary of the Standards is as follows: Nos.1-286 (hexagonal dash 1910-23); Nos.287-664 (round dash 1898-1910); Nos.665-685 (hexagonal dash 1923-24); Nos.686-1000 (round dash 1898-1910); Nos.1039, 1040, 1050, 1051, 1088 (hexagonal dash 1924).

A further 68 cars dating from 1904 to 1919 were acquired in 1923 with the take-over of the Paisley District Tramways and these became Nos.1001-38, 1041-49 and 1052-72. Another 15 had arrived the previous year (Nos.1073-87) when the Airdrie & Coatbridge Tramways were

absorbed. Not all of them entered passenger service with Glasgow Corporation. Prototype single-deck bogie car No.1089 was built at Coplawhill Works in 1926. Although reminiscent of the original 'room and kitchen' trams, it owed more to current American practice, but proved

unsatisfactory for the Glasgow system. Instead of developing this design, the Corporation decided to modernise the Standards and ordered 51 maximum-traction double-deck bogie cars which were delivered in 1927-28. Because of the pressure of work at Coplawhill all but two of them were built by outside

Four streamlined four-wheel cars were built in 1940 as potentially less expensive successors to the Coronations, but cost savings proved negligible. Before this project was abandoned, a similar vehicle was constructed in place of Standard No.6 which received a direct hit in Nelson Street during the Blitz of March 1941. The new No.6 was known as the 'coffin' because of its shape, the fate of its predecessor, its partial destruction in the Newlands depot fire of 1948 and its involvement in at least one fatal accident. In 1951 all five experimental cars were sent to Elderslie Depot for peak hour services to and from Renfrew Ferry, but when the Paisley system closed in 1957 they saw no further use. In this view, No.6 traverses Paisley Cross on 13th January 1956.

The hundred Cunarders were basically a post-war version of the Coronations, although there were detail differences - notably the front-end styling. On 16th April 1960, No.1328 ascends Albert Drive on route 3 from Mosspark to Park Road near the University. It takes precedence over one of the 35ft long single-deck trolleybuses on service 108 from Mount Florida to Shieldhall, which replaced tram route 12 in 1958. Almost hidden by the trees in the left background is 'The Knowe' a house built by Alexander 'Greek' Thomson in the early 1850s.

suppliers, namely R&Y Pickering (Wishaw), Brush (Loughborough) and Hurst, Nelson (Motherwell). Nos.1090-1140 were fitted with running gear from the Kilmarnock Engineering Company (actually English Electric by then), hence the nickname 'Kilmarnock Bogies'. Unfortunately they were prone to derailment, which confined them to the relatively straight east-west routes.

Following persistent complaints about the bucking and swaying ride of the Standards, Glasgow Corporation decided to authorise the construction of a revolutionary class of new bogie cars. The first of these 152 sleek, stylish and comfortable trams appeared in 1937 and delivery was completed in 1941. They were appropriately called 'Coronations' after the main national event during their inaugural year. Ever since, Nos.1141-1292 have been widely regarded as the finest street vehicles ever. However, they were expensive to build, so lightweight four-wheel cars Nos.1001-1004, with the same streamlined bodywork, were constructed in 1940 as possible successors. A similar vehicle, No.6, entered service in 1943, having been built to replace a Standard destroyed in an air raid a couple of years previously. Cost savings were negligible and the design was not perpetuated.

An experimental single-ended bogie car, No.1005, appeared in 1947 sporting a three-tone blue livery, but it was eventually rebuilt as a conventional streamliner. The pedigree of the Coronations could not be denied, so another hundred cars designated 'Cunarders' but very similar to their predecessors were turned out between 1948 and 1952. These became Nos.1293 to 1392. With the impending closure of Liverpool's tram system, Glasgow acquired 46 elegant bogie cars from Merseyside in 1953-55. The 'Green Goddesses' became Nos.1006-16, 1018-38, 1041-49 and 1052-56 in the Glasgow fleet. Finally, Coplawhill turned out six new modified Coronations in 1954 built on bogies from Liverpool cars destroyed in that city's Green Lane Depot fire. Nos.1393-98 heralded the end of a magnificent era of tram building in Glasgow.

During 1953 and 1955, Glasgow purchased two batches of Green Goddess bogie trams from Liverpool Corporation, these distinctive vehicles having been built at that city's Edge Lane Works in 1936-37. They cost a reasonable £500 apiece, but were not well received in Glasgow. Most of the 46 cars were in poor condition and their greater width restricted them to certain routes. No.1036 (ex-Liverpool No.891) descends Hope Street and crosses St. Vincent Street, working service 29 from Maryhill to Broomhouse on 30th March 1960.

In the midst of Saturday afternoon traffic on 6th June 1959, Standard No.139 turns out of Renfield Street into Sauchiehall Street, bound for Springburn on service 25. In 1872 Glasgow's first trams from St. George's Cross to Eglinton Toll used the sharp curve in the foreground. The Corporation Transport Offices, well known as 46 Bath Street, occupied the tall building to the left of the Coronation on route 3.

CHAPTER 3
CITY CENTRE

Although Glasgow was a significant place in medieval times and still has the cathedral and Provands Lordship as reminders of those distant days, it is essentially a creation of the Victorian era. The population grew from less than a quarter of a million in 1840 to over a million by the turn of the century, largely as a result of the burgeoning docks, shipyards, ironworks, engineering factories and railways. To accommodate the influx of workers and their families, row upon row of tenements grew up. Some blocks were grim and basic, but many were elegant buildings helping to give Glasgow its unique character. However, the real gems of Victorian architecture were in the city centre.

During the 1850s Alexander 'Greek' Thomson built several dignified terraces and numerous churches, the classical towers of which punctuated the city skyline. The iron-framed Gardner's Warehouse in Jamaica Street was a revolutionary design and its completion in 1856

marked the beginning of a massive wave of reconstruction which transformed inner Glasgow. Hundreds of fine buildings appeared, perhaps the most notable being the sumptuous City Chambers of 1888 which dominated George Square. During the late 1890s and early 1900s, the brilliant and highly original creations of Charles Rennie Mackintosh added further to the architectural flavour of the city.

A procession of seven tartan-liveried horse trams operated by

Andrew Menzies ran from St. George's Cross to Eglinton Toll via Great Western Road, Cambridge Street, Sauchiehall Street, Renfield Street, Union Street, Jamaica Street, Glasgow Bridge, Bridge Street and Eglinton Street on 19th August 1872. They proceeded 'amid the cheers of the multitude' and the return journey was accomplished in just thirteen minutes. *The Glasgow Herald* declared that 'this new method of conveyance will run omnibuses off the street' and Menzies remarked that 'a working man coming to the city in one of these cars will feel as if he were in an easy chair'.

In the shadow of the events on that summer day, a number of other lines were nearing completion. Before the end of 1872 trams were running along Sauchiehall Street to the Crescents in the West End, from Trongate to Bridgeton in the East End and from Renfield Street to St. Vincent Place. The Jamaica Street - Trongate connection along the eastern part of Argyle Street was completed during 1873, as were the

During the 1950s trams were often accused of clogging the streets and impeding the progress of other vehicles. Nowadays, of course, private cars are by far the worst culprits when it comes to congestion. However, this motorist in upper Renfield Street during the evening rush hour of 1st August 1957 was no doubt cursing the procession of trams. Coronation No.1181 on service 5 from Holmlea Road to Kelvinside survived until the end of the system in September 1962, but trams disappeared from Renfield Street on 4th June 1960 with the withdrawal of service 3.

The line along Argyle Street and Trongate from Jamaica Street to Candleriggs saw its first horse trams in 1873. Almost ninety years later, Standards Nos.296 and 288 are virtually bumper to bumper near Glassford Street as they head east on service 15 for Garrowhill and service 26 for Farme Cross respectively, on 2nd August 1960. The Coronation is bound for Baillieston.

routes from St. Vincent Place to Dennistoun via George Square and Duke Street, and Jamaica Street to Anderston Cross via the western part of Argyle Street. In 1874 a link opened through Cowcaddens between the original St. George's Cross route and Sauchiehall Street.

After this hectic two year construction programme authorised by the original Tramways Act, there was a period of consolidation during which the horse cars established themselves as the principal means of public transport in Glasgow. Medium and long distance travellers used the railways. This was reflected by the opening of St. Enoch and Central

An early evening scene at Glasgow Cross on 10th May 1960. Homeward-bound workers wait for Standard No.177 to turn in Trongate on a service 15 'short working' for Baillieston as a train of empty stock crosses Gallowgate bridge in the background, on the City of Glasgow Union Railway. Other people were no doubt heading for Glasgow Cross station on the Central Low Level line; its entrance can be seen immediately left of the tram.

In 1874 a line opened from the original route east of St. George's Cross to Sauchiehall Street via the Cowcaddens. Mid-way along this erstwhile haunt of the horse trams, Standard No.157 reverses in Maitland Street lye on a service 31 short working from Lambhill on 14th June 1957. In the background a trolleybus turns into Hope Street, where the Theatre Royal is now the home of Scottish opera.

stations in the heart of the city during 1876 and 1879 respectively. However, the success of the trams soon resulted in more tracks being laid. The somewhat angular connection from George Square to Argyle Street via Ingram Street and Glassford Street came in 1880. This was followed by the route from Mitchell Street to Springburn via West Nile Street and Parliamentary Road, and the route from Renfield Street to Kelvin Bridge via Bothwell Street, both of them commencing in 1886. The line along High Street and Saltmarket through Glasgow Cross came shortly afterwards. By 1898, when the first electric trams began running from Mitchell Street to Springburn, the city centre network was well established. However, over the next couple of years it was transformed by the installation of heavier rails and overhead wires with their attendant poles. As more

Horse trams came to Bothwell Street with the opening of the line from Mitchell Street to St. George's Cross and Kelvinside in 1886. It paralleled earlier routes along Sauchiehall Street and Argyle Street to the north and south respectively. On 9th June 1960, Standard No.97 on a service 18 evening rush hour working uses Douglas Street crossover to return to Springburn as Coronation No.1240, bound from Burnside to Springburn, waits to follow it. In the background is the massive, gothic style Christian Institute (or YMCA) which was built in stages from 1877 and demolished in 1980.

lines opened in the inner and outer suburbs, the central area tracks had to cope with an increasing number of trams. The three east-west routes proved adequate but most north-south services had to use Renfield Street. Consequently, tracks were laid from Cowcaddens along Hope Street and Oswald Street in 1927 to relieve the pressure. They continued across King George V Bridge, opened that year, to join the original route along Bridge Street at its junction with Eglinton Street.

Because of the sheer number of tram routes which passed through the centre of Glasgow, it would be somewhat tedious to describe the sequence of withdrawals in narrative form. However, the following table shows the date of the last scheduled service along most city streets, together with a list of routes which once traversed them. Individual service closures are mentioned in subsequent chapters.

Date	Street	Services
19th February 1949	High Street	2. 19
19th February 1949	Saltmarket	2, 10, 19 (10 diverted to London Road)
4th July 1953	Glassford Street	11, 13
4th July 1953	West Nile Street	11, 13, 23 (23 diverted to Renfield Street)
15th November 1958	Oswald Street	4, 22, 27, 40
4th June 1960	Jamaica Street	3, 5, 8, 14, 21, 24, 25, 31, 32
4th June 1960	Renfield Street	1, 3, 5, 8, 14. 23, 24, 25, 30, 31, 32
4th June 1960	Sauchiehall Street	1, 3, 5, 6, 14, 16, 24, 25, 31, 33
4th June 1960	Union Street	3, 5, 8, 14, 21, 24, 25, 31, 32
5th November 1960	George Square	1, 13, 23, 30
5th November 1960	St. Vincent Street	1, 15, 23, 30
3rd June 1961	Bothwell Street	10, 17, 18, 21, 36, 40
3rd June 1961	Hope Street	4, 10, 17, ,18, 21, 22, 27, 36, 40
1st September 1962	Argyle Street	9, 10, 15, 17, 18, 26, 29, 36
1st September 1962	Trongate	9, 10, 15, 17, 18, 26, 29, 36

The evening rush hour is in full swing on 22nd May 1957 as Standard cars Nos.369 and 272, on short workings of service 15 from Baillieston and service 1 from Dalmarnock respectively, turn at Wellington Street lye in St. Vincent Street. The tall building behind the rear of No.369 is the Art Nouveau 'Hatrack' dating from the turn of the century and having a frontage just ten yards wide. Dominating the other car is the massive 1920s neo-classical Bank of Scotland edifice. Both structures survive.

A young lady appears to be paying homage to Standard No.388 as it passes Central Station and crosses Argyle Street, from Hope Street to Oswald Street, on 4th September 1958. More prosaically, she was probably keeping a careful eye on the setts in the roadway, which could trip the unwary. This route was a relative latecomer, opening in 1927. Service 22 ran between Lambhill and Crookston until it was replaced by buses from 15th November 1958.

Glasgow's Trams

Cunarder No.1306, on service 10 from London Road to Kelvinside via Charing Cross, climbs away from Kelvin Bridge and heads along Great Western Road near the end of its journey. It was 3rd June 1960, the penultimate day of route 10. Steam trains on the Central Low Level line still ran below the road at this time. Buckingham Terrace in the background still retains much of its original elegance today.

CHAPTER 4
WEST END

St. George's Cross, Charing Cross and Anderston Cross have long marked the start of the West End, and since 1971 the M8 motorway has cut a swathe past these once important road junctions, emphasising the western limit of the city centre. The West End as a whole is a long wedge, roughly bounded by the River Kelvin and Forth & Clyde Canal to the north and precisely defined by the River Clyde in the south. It embraces Hillhead, Partick, Hyndland, Kelvinside, Anniesland, Scotstoun, Knightswood and Yoker.

Two main thoroughfares pass through this part of Glasgow. Dumbarton Road, which follows on from Argyle Street, runs close to the Clyde. It was the main road to the north side of the Firth of Clyde and a gateway to the Western Highlands, but its hinterland at Partick and Scotstoun became dominated by tenements and riverside industry

during the nineteenth century. Great Western Road, much of it straight as an arrow, was laid out during the early 1830s as a direct approach from Dumbarton. Some of the city's most fashionable houses grew up around it, notably the magnificent crescents of the Park and the grand terraces designed by 'Greek' Thomson.

The West End has several attractive open spaces, most notably Kelvingrove Park, the Botanic Gardens and Victoria Park. It also includes Glasgow University, Kelvin Hall and the Western Infirmary. Along its southern fringe, shipyards, docks and factories lined the bank of the Clyde all the way from Yoker to Anderston. At Finnieston Quay, locomotives built by the North British Locomotive Company and destined for export throughout the world were lifted aboard shops by the mightiest of cranes.

Another feature of the West End was the intense network of suburban railways built by the Caledonian and North British companies.

Botanic Gardens on the Central Low Level line has been variously described as a 'station with knobs on' and 'not looking out of place in the Kremlin'! Although closed in 1939, it found various uses subsequently, and was a nightclub when destroyed by fire in 1970. On 16th January 1960, Standard No.288 working route 30 from Blairdardie to Dalmarnock via St. George's Cross heads east along Great Western Road as a suburban train passes below.

Standard No.190 heads out of town along Great Western Road on service 1 from Dalmarnock to Scotstoun West, 16th January 1960. Elegant Kelvinside station on another arm of the Central Low Level line is on the left. It closed in 1942 and eventually became 'Carriages' restaurant, only to be gutted by fire recently. Fortunately the building was

Services emanated from Central Low Level and Queen Street Low Level stations respectively, the lines passing above or beneath the tram routes in numerous places. Overbridges and station buildings provide points of interest in several of the views in this chapter. Some of the suburban routes, in fact, have outlived the trams by several decades.

St. George's Cross saw the first

horse trams in Glasgow, during 1872, and by the end of that year rails had been laid along Great Western Road as far as Bellhaven Terrace near Botanic Gardens. Also during 1872, a line opened from Sauchiehall Street to Whiteinch via Charing Cross and Dumbarton Road. The Argyle Street line to Kelvingrove via Anderston Cross followed shortly afterwards. In 1880 the tracks along Great Western

Road were extended from Bellhaven Terrace to Hyndland Road and had reached Anniesland by 1905. Knightswood was served from the early 1920s and a further extension to Blairdardie came as late as 1949. The Dumbarton Road route stretched as far as Scotstoun and Yoker by the turn of the century, then ventured beyond the city boundary to Clydebank and Dalmuir in 1903/04. Eventually there

Having negotiated Anniesland Cross, Standard No.1051 heads east along Great Western Road towards Botanic Gardens while working service 30 to Dalmarnock, on 16th January 1960. The large bowstring girder bridge taking the Queen Street Low Level line into Anniesland station dates from 1937, when the road was widened.

Standard No.132 at the Blairdardie terminus of route 30 in Great Western Road on 16th May 1956. Relatively modern houses in the background and reserved tracks for the trams indicate that this was a late extension. In fact it was the last major addition to the Glasgow system, opening from Knightswood on 31st July 1949. Service 30 was withdrawn on 12th March 1960, but the grass-grown central reservation waits (hopefully not in vain) for a modern light transit system.

was even a connection with the Dumbarton Tramways, which had a line to Balloch on distant Loch Lomond (Chapter 8).

During Edwardian times there was a fair amount of tramway 'infill' between the Dumbarton Road and Great Western Road arteries in the wake of electrification. A couple of links had already materialised during 1886, in the form of the routes from Charing Cross to St George's Cross and along Woodlands Road to Kelvin Bridge. The Byers Road connection was operational by 1905. From 1907 to 1910 rails were installed in Highburgh Road, Hyndland Road, Clarence Drive, Crow Road and Eldon Street (for the University). The Hyndland Road tracks, which ended outside the North British Railway terminus at Hyndland, were extended

On the warm and sunny evening of 5th September 1959 there was an animated scene where Argyle Street merged with Dumbarton Road. The occasion was the prestigious Scottish Industries Exhibition at Kelvin Hall, just off to the left. Coronation No.1251 heads east on service 16 from Scotstoun to Springburn via Charing Cross, with the Victorian Baronial facade of Western Infirmary forming a fine backdrop beyond the River Kelvin. This particular car was destroyed in the Dalmarnock depot fire of March 1961, the same month in which service 16 was replaced by buses. The Glasgow Museum of Transport now occupies part of Kelvin Hall.

to Great Western Road in 1924. A contemporary development was the link from Anniesland to Scotstoun.

In 1955 the West End system was still complete, apart from a short stub from Finnieston to Stobcross Ferry which closed in 1927 and the line along North Street near Charing Cross, removed during 1945. However, the 'infill' between Partick, Anniesland and Hillhead was largely obliterated with the withdrawal of route 5 in 1957 and routes 17 and 24 during 1958. The University cars (service 3) ceased in 1960, as did routes 1, 10 and 30 along Great Western Road. Finally, Dumbarton Road lost service 16 in 1961, followed by 9 and 26 in 1962.

Right. In evening sunshine on 19th July 1961, Coronation No.1165 heads along Dumbarton Road just west of Partick Cross while working route 26 from Dalmarnock to Clydebank. The entrance to Partick Cross Subway station is in the tenement block to the left of the tram. Glasgow had over a hundred picture houses and was said to be the most cinema-conscious city in Britain. One of the less opulent examples was the Western which had become something of a flea pit when in closed in 1966!

Below. By chance, a variety of transport came together at Partick on the afternoon of 6th June 1960. Kilmarnock bogie No.1131 heads west on service 26 from Burnside to Scotstoun, a Corporation AEC Regent is bound for the city centre, a Central SMT Leyland PD2 is destined for Helensburgh and a steam-hauled suburban train from Queen Street Low Level rolls into Partick Hill station. The triangle of tram lines in the foreground marked the entrance to Partick depot.

On the quiet Sunday afternoon of 6th March 1960, Standard No.108 turns from Kingsway into Dumbarton Road, photographed from the embankment carrying the Central Low Level line near Scotstoun West station. Service 1, which worked from Springfield Road and Dalmarnock to Dalmuir via George Square and Great Western Road, was replaced by buses a week later. High-rise flats now occupy the parkland in the background.

It was foggy on the afternoon of Saturday 16th November 1957, as Standard No.105 passed Hillhead Subway station in Byres Road. Route 5 ran from Hyndland station, Kelvinside, to Holmlea Road (Clarkston until trolleybuses took over in 1953) on the South Side. In the West End it formed a circle from Byres Road by using Highburgh Road, Hyndland Road and Great Western Road, or vice versa. Cosmopolitan Byres Road, the haunt of Glasgow University students, is almost unchanged today.

Standard No.83 whines along Clarence Drive towards Broomhill Cross en route from Langside to Anniesland on 15th March 1958. This was the last day of tram service 24 prior to its replacement by bus service 44, a route almost unique in Glasgow in that it has loyally followed the course taken by its predecessors for the last forty years. Crow Road station on the Central Low Level system closed in 1960.

At Glasgow Cross the transition between the city centre and the East End was abrupt. Within a few hundred yards, the large stores and commercial premises of Argyle Street and Trongate gave way to tenements and small shops in Gallowgate and London Road. Overlooked by the spiky tower of the Tollbooth, Standard No.22 working service 15 from Anderston Cross to Baillieston crosses the divide and heads east along Gallowgate, on 2nd August 1960. The City of Glasgow Union Railway runs over the lattice girder bridge. From 1871 Gallowgate had a station in Molendinar Street off to the right, served by frequent 'bus trains' between Govan and the North Side. It closed in 1902 when the trains surrendered to tramway competition, a move which shocked railway companies throughout Britain.

CHAPTER 5
EAST END

High Street and Saltmarket, which meet at Glasgow Cross, effectively form the eastern boundary of the city centre. This area was the heart of medieval Glasgow, but as the port developed, commercial activity tended to move further west. For the purposes of this book, the East End is bounded by Duke Street and Shettleston Road to the north and the sweeping loops of the River Clyde to the south. It incorporates the districts of Calton, Camlachie, Bridgeton, Dalmarnock, Parkhead, Shettleston and Tollcross.

Two main roads diverge at Glasgow Cross. Gallowgate heads almost due east to Parkhead Cross where it splits into Tollcross Road and Westmuir Street, the latter leading to Shettleston Road. London Road heads south east through Bridgeton Cross where Dalmarnock Road veers away to the south. This was one of the poorest parts of the city. Initially, both Gallowgate and London Road passed through areas crammed with particularly bleak tenements.

Commerce and industry dominated the East End. Near High Street there was a sprawl of railway goods yards and depots, whilst a little further east the city's huge

cattle market occupied many acres between Duke Street and Gallowgate. This part of Glasgow also had several ironworks, notably the mighty Parkhead Forge. To the south, a forest of chimneys reared up from Dalmarnock Power Station. Fortunately tenement dwellers could escape to a number of open spaces, the most famous and popular of which was Glasgow Green. Even this was overlooked by

Templeton's Carpet Factory, but in this case the exotic facade based on the Doge's Palace in Venice was a positive asset. Another significant place in the East End, indeed a shrine to many, was the Parkhead stadium of Glasgow Celtic Football Club.

The Caledonian and North British suburban railways which were a feature of the West End also passed through the eastern part of the city. The former tunnelled beneath London Road and Dalmarnock Road as far as Parkhead and Dalmarnock respectively, whilst the latter ran parallel to Gallowgate and crossed Duke Street near its junction with Shettleston Road, before heading off towards Airdrie.

During 1872 a horse tramway was laid from Candleriggs, off Trongate, to Bridgeton Cross via London Road. The line along Gallowgate from Glasgow Cross to Bellgrove and Camlachie Burn followed in 1873. This was extended further east to Camlachie Toll in 1875 and the Bridgeton Cross tracks explored more of London Road during the same year. Camlachie Toll to Parkhead opened in 1880, followed by the branch along Dalmarnock Road from Bridgeton Cross in 1882. Powers to extend the

On 2nd June 1960, Standard No.585 enters Whitevale lye in Rowchester Street, Camlachie, on a short working of service 15 from Anderston Cross. The lye (a Scottish word for a short siding) took its name from Whitevale horse tram depot which once stood nearby. Another Standard car waits to proceed west along Gallowgate towards Calton and Glasgow Cross. Route 15 ceased on 10th March 1962.

A typical East End scene at the Parkhead end of Gallowgate, the tenements standing shoulder to shoulder with equally drab post-war council blocks. Well-laden Standard trams Nos.229 and 61 brought a touch of colour to the otherwise grey evening of 2nd June 1960. The former is on service 29 from Maryhill to Tollcross (withdrawn 21st October 1961) whilst the latter is working route 15, from Anderston Cross to Baillieston.

Dalmarnock Road route were obtained in 1899, less than a year after the first electric trams ran to Springburn, and the line duly reached Rutherglen in 1902, Cambuslang in 1903 and Burnside in 1908. By 1905 electric trams were running along Duke Street to Parkhead, then on to Shettleston and Tollcross. The extension to Baillieston came in 1906 and Uddingston was served from 1907. A certain amount of

infill between the radial routes also took place. The line along Abercromby Street and Bellgrove Street between London Road and Duke Street was in place by 1905 and the tracks following Springfield Road from Parkhead Cross to Dalmarnock had been laid by 1911. The extension along London Road to Auchenshuggle came in 1922.

Early withdrawals in the East End were covered by other services and

no route mileage was lost: No.35, the Dennistoun/Rutherglen Circular, went in 1949; No.34 from Auchenshuggle to Anderston Cross finished in 1952; No.36 between Parkhead and Kelvinside expired in 1953. Then there was a lull until the 'infill' routes vanished from the map. Route 7 from Millerston to Bellahouston was withdrawn in 1958, so trams ceased to run along Bellgrove Street. Services 1

Parkhead Cross was the tramway hub of Glasgow's East End and even boasted a pointsman's box. On 5th March 1960 Standard car No.83 turns from Gallowgate into Springfield Road, on Route 30 from Blairdardie to Dalmarnock via St. George's Cross. In the background a Coronation stands in Duke Street. Service 30 ceased on 12th March 1960.

An almost small-town scene at Tollcross on 30th May 1960. Standard No.156 sways along Tollcross Road past Anwoth Street which leads to the little-known Glasgow suburb called Egypt. The car is westbound on service 29 from Broomhouse to Maryhill via Normal School.

and 30, Dalmarnock - Dalmuir West and Dalmarnock - Blairdardie respectively, finished in March 1960 rendering the rails along Springfield Road redundant. June of the same year saw the finale of route 10 from London Road to Kelvinside and No.23 between Baillieston and Maryhill followed five months later.

The radial routes lost their services over the next two years. No.18 from Burnside to Springburn via Dalmarnock Bridge was withdrawn in June 1961. Trams ceased to run along Tollcross Road during October 1961 when route 29 from Tollcross to Maryhill finished, whilst Shettleston Road lost its cars in March 1962 with the abandonment of service 15 between Baillieston and Anderston Cross. Dalmarnock Road became rail-less after route 26 from Dalmarnock (Burnside earlier) to Dalmuir West ended in June 1962. The very end came in September 1962 when the last No.9 trams between Auchenshuggle and Dalmuir West plied along London Road.

Standard No.556, westbound on service 1 from Dalmarnock to Scotstoun West, heads along Duke Street on 5th March 1960. The stark little building to the left is Duke Street station entrance on the City of Glasgow Union Railway. Route 1 was abandoned a week later, on 12th March 1960.

The grim face of heavy industry in the East End during winter is amply portrayed in this view of two Standards heading west along Duke Street, on 5th March 1960. Both are destined for the city centre and Scotstoun West on route 1 from Dalmarnock, the leading car being No.394. Parkhead Forge dominates the scene and the girder bridge carried the Airdrie - Queen Street Low Level line.

During the sunny early evening of 15th May 1961, Standard No.585 heads east along London Road on a service 9 rush hour working from the West End. The London Road entrance to Bridgeton Cross station on the Central Low Level line beckons from the right. A wall of tenements on Heron Street in the distance overlooks the ex-Caledonian suburban railways diverging to Rutherglen via Dalmarnock and Carmyle via Parkhead respectively. Route 9 ceased to operate on 1st September 1962.

Virtually a 'tram sandwich' in the East End on the morning of 24th September 1960, with railways both above and below the street-level tracks. Standard No.169 heads east along Dalmarnock Road towards Burnside on service 26 from Dalmuir (abandoned 2nd June 1962). The car is about to pass beneath the Rutherglen - London Road branch, opened in 1877, and has just traversed a section of street laid on top of the Central Low Level line tunnel, completed during 1895. Dalmarnock station on the underground route, prominent on the left, replaced high level passenger facilities off to the right.

Dalmarnock Road was lined with drab tenements typical of Glasgow's East End, and at Springfield Road crossover on 5th March 1960 Standard cars Nos.235 and 121 looked forlorn amid a chilly mist shrouding the Clyde. One of the chimneys of nearby Dalmarnock Power Station is barely visible though the murk. No.235 is ready to work service 1 from Springfield Road to Scotstoun West, whilst No.121 nears the end of its long trek from Blairdardie to Dalmarnock on route 30.

Cheerful autumn sunshine on the morning of 24th September 1960 did little to liven up woebegone Kilmarnock Bogie No.1122 as it crossed the Clyde at Dalmarnock Bridge on service 26 from Scotstoun to Burnside. Despite the tenements on Allan Street in the background, this was very much an industrial area. The chimneys of Dalmarnock Power Station dominated the scene and Downiebrae Road, in the right foreground, led to a complex of heavy engineering works.

Standard No.532, forming a short working of service 18 to Maitland Street, Cowcaddens, heads down Maryhill Road past Ye Olde Tramcar Vaults near St. George's Cross on 30th August 1960. Route 18, Springburn to Burnside in full, was withdrawn on 3rd June 1961.

CHAPTER 6
NORTH SIDE

Dobbie's Loan, just beyond the site of Buchanan Street Station, more or less marks the northern boundary of central Glasgow. From here, the North Side extends out in an elongated diamond shape, some six miles wide and two miles deep. It encompasses the whole area north of the River Kelvin and Duke Street as far as the city boundary. Maryhill, Ruchill, Lambhill, Possil, Port Dundas, Springburn, Garngad, Provanmill and Millerston are the districts concerned.

There are five radial roads - from west to east, Maryhill Road, Balmore Road, Springburn Road, Royston Road and Cumbernauld Road. This is quite a complex part of Glasgow. It had its fair share of tenements, but they tended to cluster around focal points such as Garngad and Springburn rather than spread out from the centre, as was largely the case in the East and West Ends. The North Side had plenty of open spaces, although many of these formed gaps between industrial and housing areas, Dawsholm Park being a notable exception. There were also

four major hospitals, all within a couple of miles of Springburn.

A unique feature of the North Side was the Forth & Clyde Canal and its associated branch to Port Dundas. In no less than three places - Maryhill, Ruchill and Port Dundas - trams passed beneath solid stone aqueducts where the waterways crossed roads. A major influence on the area north east of the city centre was the presence of two early railways, the pioneering Garnkirk & Glasgow, which formed the basis of the line out of Buchanan Street, and the Edinburgh & Glasgow trunk route into Queen Street.

A massive concentration of heavy engineering directly related to these railways developed in an area of less than a square mile around Springburn. The Caledonian and North British had their main works at St. Rollox and Cowlairs respectively, whilst the North British Locomotive Company had two factories nearby. In fact, almost certainly, Springburn was the largest locomotive building complex in the world during the early part of this century. Nevertheless, a couple of other industrial establishments made a far greater visual impact. One was Tennents chemical works, a byword for noxious fumes for many years. The other was Glasgow Corporation's Pinkston Power Station, which supplied electricity to the tramway system from 1901.

The North Side gained its trams somewhat later

At the close of the evening rush hour on 10th August 1960, Standard No.77 nears the end of its service 29 duty, from Broomhouse in the East End to Maryhill Depot. The car is passing Maryhill Barracks, home of the Highland Light Infantry, and Maryhill Central station on the Central Low Level line. Route 29 finished on 21st October 1961. The station site is now occupied by a supermarket and the barracks has been replaced by new housing.

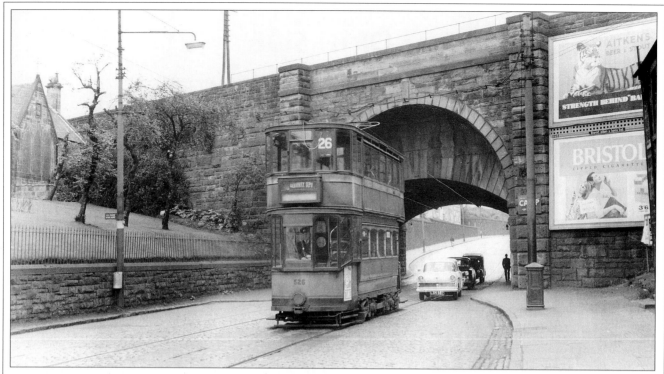

Occasionally, Glasgow's trams managed to confuse their passengers. On 10th August 1960, Standard No.526 emerges from beneath the Forth & Clyde Canal aqueduct across Maryhill Road on a somewhat odd working to Dalmarnock Depot. Furthermore, it is displaying service number 26 - normally allocated to the Scotstoun - Dalmarnock route which plied Dumbarton Road in the West End!

than either the West End or East End and the network was far less dense. However, no fewer than eighteen routes (half the total) still served the area in 1949. Initially, construction was confined to Maryhill Road and its vicinity. During 1880 a line opened along Maryhill Road from St. George's Cross to the junction with Garscube Road and this was extended to Maryhill itself in 1881. The link from Cowcaddens to the Maryhill route via

Garscube Road came in 1882, followed by the connection from St. George's Cross to Garscube Road along St. George's Road in 1886. A line from Mitchell Street in the city centre to Springburn via Parliamentary Road, St. Rollox and Springburn Road also opened in 1886. This acquired great significance in 1898 when it became the first route to be electrified.

By 1905, following the success

of this venture, several new lines were in operation on the North Side. Possil Road was linked to Springburn via both Keppochhill Road and Hawthorn Street, an extension of the Springburn tracks led to Bishopbriggs and a line ran along Alexandra Parade and Cumbernauld Road to Riddrie. By 1911, Bilsland Drive, Lambhill and Garngad were served. Two more extensions came in the 1920s - Riddrie to Millerston and Garngad to

In late afternoon sunshine on 30th October 1959, a day before the demise of service 6, Cunarder No.1315 passes along Parliamentary Road en route from Riddrie to Scotstoun. The old soot-begrimed railway buildings on the left, incorporating former stables, housed the Scottish Region Audit Office at the time. Not only have the tram and Audit Office passed into history, but 'Parly Road' itself is no more.

Passing a cliff-like wall of tenements in the St. Rollox district, Standard No.195 descends the lower part of Springburn Road on 6th June 1959, the last day of route 25 from Bishopbriggs and Springburn to Carnwadric and Rouken Glen. Glasgow's first electric tram service passed this point on 13th October 1898.

A variety of trams at Springburn, the home of locomotive building, on 3rd March 1958. Standard No.161, on service 27 from Springburn to Shieldhall, and Coronation No.1187 on route 18A from Springburn to Shawfield, stand at Hawthorn Street crossover as a Cunarder heads along Springburn Road towards Bishopbriggs on service 25. Routes 27 and 18A were withdrawn on 15th March 1958 and 3rd June 1961 respectively.

Service 16 from Scotstoun approached Springburn along Keppochhill Road and terminated at Elmvale Street. Seen there on 8th March 1958 are Standard No.44 and Cunarder No.1310. Route 16 expired three years later, on 11th March 1961.

Coronation No.1277, on service 16 from Scotstoun to Keppochhill Road and Springburn, passes under the aqueduct carrying the Port Dundas branch of the Forth & Clyde Canal across Possil Road. The date is 23rd June 1960.

Provanmill. Although the latter filled an obvious gap on the map, it proved uneconomic and was quite short-lived. Maryhill to Canniesburn Toll opened in 1922 and Hillfoot was reached the following year. However, the tracks did not reach Milngavie until 1934 because of objections from the London & North Eastern Railway, which already served the town.

The North Side saw two notable withdrawals as early as 1949, when route 19 from Springburn to Netherlee and route 2 from Provanmill to Polmadie were replaced by buses. Services 11 and 13 from Milngavie to Sinclair Drive and Glasgow Cross respectively finished in 1951 and 1953, again respectively. There was a major onslaught in 1958 when trams 4, 7, 22, 27 and 32 disappeared from the city streets. Routes 4, 27 and 32 from Springburn to the South Side had been instrumental in killing off the Glasgow & South Western 'Bus Trains' half a century earlier. During 1959 services 6, 8, 25, 31 and 33 were withdrawn. They were a mixed bunch, including the Springburn Circular and two long runs from Millerston and Bishopbriggs to Rouken Glen in the leafy hills well south of the city. Route 23 out of Maryhill finished in 1960, followed by service 16 along Keppochhill Road early the following year. Springburn, which saw the first electric trams, became the preserve of buses when route 18 finished in the summer of 1961. Finally, service 29 from Maryhill to Tollcross was withdrawn in autumn 1961, eighty years after rails first ventured into the North Side streets.

Apart from a Corporation Leyland bus, the trams on service 16 were probably the most modern items in Keppochhill Road on 9th June 1960. Coronation No.1151 was built in 1938 and Cunarder No.1322 dated from 1950. The buildings on the right, housing a printing firm, the Crown Billiard Saloon and the Cowlairs Labour Party, was originally a horse tram depot but became the first electric car shed and generating station. Springburn fire station at the corner of Springburn Road is behind the 'caurs'.

On 16th May 1961 Coronation No.1144, working service 18A from Springburn to Shawfield, passes under the bridge carrying the Ruchill Hospital railway across Bilsland Drive. Traffic over this half-mile branch from the Caledonian north side goods line at Possil Junction consisted mainly of coal for the hospital boiler house, but during World War I it was traversed by hospital trains carrying wounded soldiers from the holocaust of the trenches.

Thick fog shrouded Glasgow on 5th December 1959, poignant weather for the last day of tram services to Strachur Street terminus in Lambhill. Modified Coronation No.1397 waits to depart for Merrylee on route 31. Five Coronations and three Cunarders from Possilpark and Newlands depots worked the line for most of the day. Lambhill had also been the terminus of service 22, from Crookston, until 15th November 1958.

Persistent rain marked the demise of route 8 from Millerston to Rouken Glen on 14th March 1959. Cunarder No.1310 on the last leg of its cross-city journey from the Renfrewshire hills to Glasgow's northern suburbs whines forlornly along bleak and deserted Smithycroft Road in Riddrie. The melancholy atmosphere is accentuated by the huddle of World War II prefabs and the grim outline of Barlinnie Gaol on the left.

During the crisp early afternoon of 28th November 1959, Standard No.245 heads south along Eglinton Street on route 31 from Lambhill to Merrylee. Eglinton Street station, the first stop out of Glasgow Central, is prominent on the left, whilst a trail of smoke in the distance marks the passage of a Paisley-bound train from Glasgow St. Enoch. Service 31 was withdrawn less than a week later, on 4th December.

CHAPTER 7
SOUTH SIDE

Strictly speaking, the South Side comprises a wedge of residential suburbs south of the Clyde, spreading out from Kingston, Gorbals and Hutchesontown to Thornliebank, Clarkston and Castlemilk. However, when considering the tramway system, it is necessary to include much of the riverside development between Renfrew and Rutherglen together with the estates which grew up on land once belonging to Pollok House. This chapter therefore covers the districts of Shieldhall, Govan, Mosspark, Pollokshields, Shawlands, Pollokshaws, Langside, Govanhill, Mount Florida, Cathcart and Polmadie. Glasgow Corporation trams actually ventured out as far as Barrhead, Paisley and beyond, but these areas definitely belong to the Outer Reaches chapter.

From the four river crossings at King George V Bridge, Glasgow Bridge, Victoria Bridge and Albert Bridge, main roads radiate out through a sweep of 180 degrees. From west to east they are Govan Road, Paisley Road, Pollokshaws Road, Aikenhead Road and Rutherglen Road. Local radial routes such as Victoria Road

and Cathcart Road are significant as well, such is the complexity of the area.

The South Side of Glasgow displayed considerable contrasts, in fact more so than any of the previous three segments. Shipbuilding, heavy engineering and docks dominated the riverside west of the bridges and to some extent remains the preserve of industry today. Gorbals, the first large concentration of tenements south of the river, became a byword for slum housing - but it was a community of immense character despite the deprivation and violence. Then came a succession of fashionable Victorian and Edwardian suburbs, with superior

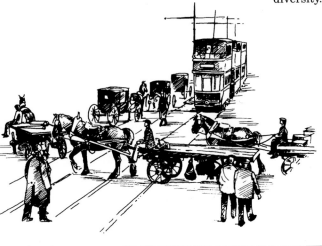

tenements and elegant villas. This was the area served by the celebrated Cathcart Circle Railway.

Still the contrasts continued. The proudly independent Burgh of Rutherglen, which has a longer history then Glasgow itself, seemed worlds apart from the vast housing schemes such as Castlemilk which developed on the periphery in the 1930s and 1950s. Open spaces such as Bellahouston Park, Pollok Grounds, Queens Park and the rural playgrounds of Rouken Glen and Cathkin Braes made this the greenest part of the city. Ibrox, home of Glasgow Rangers, and mighty Hampden Park added further to the diversity.

Horse trams began running between St. George's Cross and Eglinton Toll via Glasgow Bridge in 1872 and the short branch from Bridge Street to Paisley Road Toll opened during the same year. This spur immediately became the springing point for the Vale of Clyde Tramways to Govan and Linthouse, as well as the Ibrox Tramways to Bellahouston. Eglinton Toll to Queens Park and Langside opened in 1875-76. During 1877 the first urban

Followed by a Scotstoun-built Albion lorry, Standard No.343 passes Gorbals Cross on 2nd March 1958 working route 7 from Bellahouston to Riddrie. In pre-war years this service was identified by yellow upper deck panels and was nicknamed 'the yellow peril' as it traversed the territory of the Gorbals and Bridgeton street gangs. In reality, razor attacks were confined to members of the rival factions. Service 7 was replaced by trolleybuses on 14th June 1958.

steam trams in Great Britain were introduced on the Govan line.

There was a rapid expansion of routes during the 1880s. Eglinton Toll to Shawlands via Pollokshaws Road and Glasgow Cross to Crosshill via Albert Bridge came in 1880, followed by the Bridge Street - Gorbals Cross - Rutherglen Road lines parallel to the Clyde during 1881. An extension from Shawlands to Pollokshaws opened in 1882 and the track along Queens Drive from Crosshill was laid in 1886. Mount Florida had been reached by 1894.

Several new electric lines were in operation by 1905, notably the loop from Pollokshaws to Thornliebank and Giffnock, then back to Shawlands, the extension from Langside and Mount Florida to Cathcart, and the Trongate - Victoria Bridge - Gorbals Cross - Eglinton Toll route. A short branch to Polmadie had opened, whilst the Vale of Clyde and Ibrox Tramways had been taken over by Glasgow Corporation and extended to Renfrew (1902) and Paisley (1903) respectively.

By 1911 the Mount Florida - Govan route across the South Side had opened, Rutherglen had been linked with Gorbals and a branch extended from Eglinton Toll to Dumbreck. Cathcart to Netherlee opened in 1915 and Clarkston was reached in 1921. The Dumbreck branch ventured as far as Mosspark about the same time.

During 1949 the Polmadie

Top. **Major football matches at Hampden Park Stadium, which accommodated an astonishing 159,000 fans for a Scotland -v- England clash in 1937, demanded special arrangements on both the Cathcart Circle railway and the tramway system. On 2nd May 1956 Standards Nos.617, 779, 360, 702, 797 and 880 wait at Mount Florida terminus in Clincart Road for the homeward-bound crowds. This particular contest was between Scotland and Austria, which ended in a 1-1 draw.**

Middle. **A chill haze hung over Glasgow on 2nd January 1958 and deserted streets testified to the aftermath of New Year festivities. Standard No.212 on route 24 from Anniesland climbs Langside Road with Queen's Park and the adjacent recreation ground as a wintry backdrop. Langside terminus was alongside a monument marking the spot where Mary Queen of Scots was defeated by the Earl of Moray in 1568. This historic site lost its tram service on 15th March 1958.**

Bottom. **Despite the leafy acres of Pollok Grounds just to the west, Pollokshaws appears much the same as other outer suburbs on the South Side nowadays. However, this was once an independent Borough and the heart of the old village was still intact on 24th October 1959 as Cunarder No.1325 threaded Harriet Street on service 14 from Kelvingrove to Arden. The trams ceased exactly a week later and the street itself no longer exists.**

In one of the particularly affluent suburbs on the South Side, Standard No.152 reverses at Merrylee crossover in Kilmarnock Road on 25th June 1957. Even allowing for the vastly lower level of car ownership in those days, the lack of traffic on this fine summer evening is surprising. No doubt the situation was about to change, for when route 31 to Lambhill was withdrawn on 4th December 1959 no replacement bus service was deemed necessary.

branch closed with the withdrawal of service 2 from Provanmill and route 19 from Springburn to Netherlee ended the same year. Service 11 from Milngavie to Sinclair Drive finished in 1951 and Clarkston was the terminus of routes 5 and 13 until 1953. Otherwise, the South Side system remained intact in 1955 and could still boast thirteen services. However, 1956 saw the end of route 40 from Maryhill to Dumbreck via Govan and the service from Kelvinside to Holmlea Road, Cathcart, ended in 1957. There was an onslaught on South Side trams during 1958, mainly those serving the industrial area. Routes 24 and 27 (to Langside and Hillington Road respectively) finished in March, service 7 to Bellahouston was replaced by trolleybuses during June, tram 4 from Springburn to Hillington Road

Standard No.451 returning from Hillington Road to Govan Depot on service 4 passes Govan Cross during the evening of 3rd September 1958. Govan was one of the principal shipbuilding centres of the world and the three banks in this view are a reflection of the associated commercial activity. The tracks in the foreground emerging from Govan goods yard were used by a steeple-cab electric locomotive delivering materials to Fairfield Shipyard down the road. Stepping across the rails are a couple of 'leeries', Corporation Lighting Department employees responsible for lighting the gas lamps in tenement closes. Service 4 to Springburn was withdrawn on 6th September 1958.

'Shipyard Specials' were a feature of Govan Depot during the heyday of the Clyde shipbuilding industry. Besides starting and finishing times, there was a rush at mid-day as in this scene on 22nd March 1956, when workers from the Linthouse yard of Alexander Stephen & Son stampeded along Holmfauld Road to join Standards Nos.206, 134 and 798 bound for Govan and Cunarder No.1365 going to Bellahouston. Linthouse lye in Holmfauld Road was a lengthy affair with three crossovers. Originally it gave access to the Whiteinch ferry, but latterly accommodated peak workings of service 12 from Paisley Road Toll. It closed on 15th November 1958, followed by the shipyard itself ten years later.

ended in September and November saw the demise of route 12 (the local one from Mount Florida to Shieldhall) and route 32 to Crookston. It was the turn of residential districts in 1959. Services 8 and 25 to Rouken Glen finished in March and June respectively, while 14 (Arden) and 31 (Merrylee) ended during the autumn. Finally, route 3 to Mosspark expired in June 1960.

The south bank of the Clyde east of the bridges was also dominated by industry, but this was a particularly bleak part of the city. Coronation No.1168 stands at the Oatlands terminus of route 26 next to Shawfield Stadium, home of Clyde Football Club and greyhound racing. It was the evening of 6th August 1955, a few hours before services were withdrawn as a result of the elimination of trams from Main Street, Rutherglen. Route 26 was diverted through Dalmarnock and lasted until 2nd June 1962. Clyde FC subsequently moved and the site of their old ground is now a business park.

Route 12 from Linthouse and Paisley Road Toll to Mount Florida provided transport between the shipyards and residential areas of the South Side. Standard No.27, unusual in having tail lights, heads east past Strathbungo station on 12th April 1958. The station closed in May 1962 when 'Blue Trains' were introduced on the adjoining Cathcart Circle, but the street level building survives as a shop. Route 12 finished on 15th November 1958.

An almost timeless scene on the South Side, as late as 12th June 1958, with Standard No.751 on route 12 climbing Shields Road past a permanent way squad using the traditional pick and shovel, wheelbarrow and tar boiler. These would have been a familiar sight in horse tram days.

On 28th November 1959 Standard No.413 working route 3 from Mosspark to Park Road turns out of Maxwell Road into Eglinton Street at Eglinton Toll. The barrier on the right cutting off Pollokshaws Road was erected in 1946 to ease traffic congestion at this busy junction, resulting in the re-routing of several tram services. The parapet of the bridge spanning the main line out of Glasgow Central can just be seen to the right of the bus, whilst the building beyond it is the former St. Andrew's generating station.

A Scottish tradition was for the Provost of a town, Lord Provost in the case of cities, to be honoured with a pair of ornate lamp posts outside his or her home. This duly applied to Sir Michael Kelly who resided in Nithsdale Road, Pollokshields. The twin columns salute Coronation No.1241 en route for Mosspark on 20th April 1960. One of the lamps was removed on expiry of his term of office.

Cunarder No.1317 working service 3 from Mosspark to the University passes track repairs at a brisk pace on the reserved section alongside Mosspark Boulevard. The date is 18th May 1956. Bellahouston Park on the left was the site of the 1938 Empire Exhibition. This stretch of line opened in the early 1920s to serve a new Corporation housing scheme, one of the better of its type. Route 3 expired on 4th June 1960, but the reservation is still there, awaiting the return of the trams.

The short extension from Dalmuir to Dalmuir West was delayed for eleven years because of (often) heated discussions between Glasgow Corporation and the Caledonian Railway, concerning reconstruction of the bridge across the Forth & Clyde Canal, in order to take the trams. As it turned out, the link with the Dumbarton Tramways posed little threat to Caley outer suburban services. Standard No.876, bound for Partick in the West End, crosses the disputed swingbridge on 23rd November 1955. The waterway closed on 1st January 1963, four months after the trams ceased, and the bridge was subsequently replaced by a culvert.

In darkest Lanarkshire, well beyond the East End, the Airdrie & Coatbridge Tramways Co. began operations in 1904. It was taken over by Glasgow Corporation in 1922, and a link provided between the two systems at Baillieston. On 26th October 1955, little more than a year before the disappearance of this local tramway, Coronation No.1163 stands at the terminus of service 15 in Clark Street, Airdrie. Previously the crossover lay beyond the A73 Carlisle Road, in the background, but it had been re-positioned to ease traffic congestion.

CHAPTER 8
OUTER REACHES

On the occasion of the Glasgow Tramways Jubilee in 1922, the Convenor of the Tramways Committee claimed that, 'The policy of spreading out the Glasgow system far beyond the city boundaries has made the system what it is today - the most complete and the most successful system in the world.' If only the same could be said nowadays! At the time it was possible to travel by tram from Airdrie in the Lanarkshire Coalfield to Balloch at the southern end of Loch Lomond, albeit with changes of car en route. Even today, the same 32 mile journey by suburban electric train takes nearly an hour and a half. Most of the tramway tentacles were built by the Corporation itself, but two established systems were purchased by Glasgow. A couple of other tramways with links to the city network remained independent until closure.

Beyond the West End, Glasgow Corporation trams ventured outside the city boundary along Dumbarton Road, reaching Clydebank in 1903 and Dalmuir in 1904. However, the short extension to Dalmuir West was not completed until 1915 because of the contentious rebuilding of an opening bridge across the Forth & Clyde Canal, which was in Caledonian Railway ownership by then. At Dalmuir West there was a physical connection with the Dumbarton Tramways to Balloch, opened in 1908, although there were no through services. A branch from Clydebank to Duntocher on the slopes of the Kilpatrick Hills was completed in 1925, requiring the use of single-deck cars because of a low railway bridge spanning Kilbowie Road. The

Dumbarton system closed in 1928, service 20 from Clydebank to Duntocher was replaced by buses on 3rd December 1949, and the last tram left Dalmuir West on 1st September 1962.

Glasgow trams ventured well beyond the East End. Shettleston Road services reached Barrachnie during 1902 and Baillieston four years later. Nearby Langloan was the western terminus of the Airdrie & Coatbridge Tramways which had opened in 1904, but a physical connection had to wait until 1923, a year after the Corporation acquired this independent company. Before long, through services between Airdrie and Paisley were introduced. Uddingston, an outpost as far from the city centre as Dalmuir to the west, was reached by a lengthy extension of the Tollcross Road route in 1907. A connection was made here with the Lanarkshire Tramways, opened in 1903 to serve coalfield towns such as Bothwell. Glasgow cars also met Lanarkshire trams at Cambuslang, south of the Clyde, from 1903. One of the oddest outer suburban developments involved services along London Road.

On 6th June 1959, the last day of service 25 from Bishopbriggs to Rouken Glen and unusually sunny for such an occasion, Standard No.61 heads along Kirkintilloch Road towards Springburn. In the distance, the Campsie Fells form a hazy horizon. The tram has just crossed a bridge spanning the main line out of Queen Street station - at this point Glasgow - Edinburgh expresses were building up speed after climbing Cowlairs Incline.

The Royal Burgh of Rutherglen on the evening of 6th August 1955, with Standard No.588 at the crossover in Main Street, used by cars not proceeding to Burnside. The time is 8.45pm - some three hours later the trams had gone forever. Twenty years later, Rutherglen itself disappeared into the giant Strathclyde Region, but has since re-emerged. Perhaps the trams will re-emerge one day! The Scots Baronial style Town Hall clock tower is still a landmark for passengers travelling on the nearby West Coast Main Line.

Auchenshuggle became the terminus in 1922, but during the following year rails were laid to Mount Vernon on the Uddingston route, one of several contemporary schemes to relieve unemployment. The Auchenshuggle - Mount Vernon trams, in the event, only lasted a few weeks. Nevertheless, the moribund rails and overhead wires were revived as a wartime measure and through services from London Road to Carmyle operated from 1944 to 1952. The Lanarkshire system expired in 1931 and Glasgow trams disappeared from Airdrie in 1956. Uddingston services were cut back to Broomhouse in 1948, then Tollcross during 1960, but the Baillieston and Auchenshuggle routes survived until 1962.

The North Side extremities were relatively straightforward and involved no independent companies. In 1903 the Springburn route was extended along Kirkintilloch Road to Bishopbriggs and that remained the terminus. The Maryhill trams reached Canniesburn Toll in 1922 and Hillfoot during 1923, but as noted in Chapter 6, the final stretch to Milngavie was delayed until 1934 because of opposition from the LNER, which had an eye to its own suburban trains to the town. Tram services from Milngavie to Maryhill ceased in 1956, but the Bishopbriggs route proved more durable and lasted until 1959.

South of the river there was an extensive tramway network, as noted in Chapter 7, and Glasgow cars eventually served places well away from the city. In the south east, the Dalmarnock route was extended across the Clyde to Rutherglen in 1902 and a long branch reached Cambuslang during 1903. From Rutherglen the rails proceeded to Burnside in 1908, but a further extension to picturesque Cathkin Braes never materialised despite being proposed on several occasions. Due south of Glasgow, the loop from Pollokshaws through Thornliebank and Giffnock opened during the early years of electrification, serving estates of elegant new villas and the popular beauty spot of Rouken Glen. Just to the east, the Cathcart service was extended to Netherlee in 1915, and Clarkston during 1921. Clearly the shipyards and docks on the south bank of the Clyde provided an incentive for tramway construction, but the distant towns of Paisley and Renfrew also proved attractive. As a result, the large tract of land south west of Glasgow gained several particularly straggling routes. The Corporation took over the Vale of Clyde and Ibrox Tramways in 1896; the

Standard No.138, waiting to leave for Scotstoun in the West End, stands at Burnside terminus on 2nd November 1955. Meanwhile, the 11.10am from Glasgow Central to Kirkhill with 2-6-4T No.42246 in charge leaves Burnside station. The railway was a relatively late one, opening in 1904 just four years before the trams arrived. It now provides Burnside with a frequent electric service to the city centre, but it is almost forty years since the last 26 tram was seen here.

former was extended from Shieldhall to Renfrew in 1902, and the latter from Crookston to Paisley during 1903. From 1903 to 1910 the Paisley District Tramways developed an extensive network based on Paisley, radiating out to Renfrew and Renfrew Ferry, Abbotsinch, Kilbarchan and Rouken Glen via Barrhead.

Glasgow acquired the Paisley system in 1923 and closed the Elderslie - Kilbarchan and Paisley - Abbotsinch sections in 1932 and 1933 respectively. The single track between Glenfield on the southern outskirts of Paisley and Cross Stobs on the northern edge of Barrhead was abandoned in 1949. On 29th September 1956 the trams from Cross Stobs through Barrhead to Arden, west of Thornliebank were withdrawn. Service 21 from Glasgow to Paisley and Elderslie finished on 11th May 1957, as did service 28 linking Renfrew Ferry, Paisley and Glenfield. On the same date, route 4 was cut back from Renfrew to Hillington Road, finally ending on 6th September 1958. Service 14 from Arden to Kelvingrove finished on 1st November 1959. Elsewhere, Clarkston lost its trams in 1953 and the Burnside route was withdrawn in 1961.

On 29th September 1956, post-war Coronation No.1393, heading from Cross Stobs to the University, threads the narrow confines of Parkhouse Road as it leaves Barrhead and crosses the city boundary near Darnley. Just before midnight, this section of the former Paisley District Tramways closed when services were cut back to Arden near Rouken Glen. At one time, route 14 was a lengthy and convoluted operation connecting Milngavie with Renfrew Ferry via Pollokshaws.

The Paisley - Barrhead tramway was single track with passing places and closed in 1949. However, a short section of single track survived on route 28 in Paisley, until the local system was abandoned during 1957. It was in Weir Street, where a tenement block jutting into the roadway and the massive retaining wall of Paisley Gilmour Street station precluded double track. In this early 1950s view, Standard No.891 negotiates the constriction en route for Renfrew Ferry. Service 28 was known as the 'Goldmine' because of its equalised traffic flows. Photograph K.K. MacKay.

From 1898 to 1962 Coplawhill Works built, modernised, refurbished and maintained Glasgow's huge fleet of electric trams. It even came up with several new designs when most systems were relying on outside suppliers. Towards the end there were sad duties to perform as well, for wholesale scrapping of Standards was already underway when this photograph was taken on 17th May 1959. However, while Nos.237 and 56 were being dismantled, five Cunarders, six Coronations and two Kilmarnock Bogies were under repair. Following closure, the bulk of the massive works was demolished, although the paint shop was retained as the city's transport museum. When the collection was moved to Kelvin Hall, the renowned Tramway Theatre moved in.

CHAPTER 9
FINALE

As early as 1912, the Tramways Committee considered the possibility of purchasing motor buses for use in outlying areas, but it was rather too early for such a radical step. However, the idea returned in a more ominous form during 1924, the year when the last Standard tram was built. It was decided to introduce an experimental bus route across the city, from Monteith Row in the East End to Maryhill on the North Side. Fourteen single deckers were purchased and operations began on 8th December 1924. Other routes followed, including one from Finnieston to Stobcross Ferry in 1925 - the first tramway replacement service. The buses had solid rubber tyres which gave a particularly uncomfortable ride over the granite setts, so they did not go down well with passengers. Clearly, trams were seen as the mainstay of urban transport and the ambitious programme to recondition most of the Standard cars commenced in 1926. Nevertheless, another sixteen motor vehicles were ordered during 1927.

Thus far, bus services were largely regarded as

feeders to the tram network, but in 1927 the Tramways Committee recommended the conversion of the recently acquired Paisley and Airdrie systems to bus operation. This proposal was rejected by Glasgow Corporation in view of the financial commitment to the tramways. At the time there was severe competition from some 500 independent buses, which picked up passengers at will. The trams retaliated with low fares, typified by the slogan 'Paisley to Airdrie for 2d'. In 1928 the first Corporation double deck buses were introduced on cross-city routes serving new housing schemes, where the cost of extending the rails was prohibitive. The buses began to flourish and by 1933 over four hundred vehicles had been purchased.

Buses were operating a greater route mileage than the trams by the mid-1930s. Despite this apparent eclipse, there was clearly plenty of confidence in the future of the 'caurs', for the magnificent Coronations entered service in 1937-38 on routes serving the Empire Exhibition. A further four hundred buses were delivered from 1936 to 1942, but some of these replaced older vehicles and the overall total declined as a result of wartime fuel restrictions. In fact the trams came into their own again during the conflict, albeit with a heavy price to pay in terms of deferred maintenance. The system had recovered by 1948 and for a while the future looked bright - but all vestiges of optimism were snuffed out a decade later.

At first, Glasgow remained faithful to its cars. A hundred Cunarders were built in 1948-52, the six modified Coronations entered service in 1954 and all forty-six Green Goddesses had arrived from Liverpool by 1955. However, there had been a hint of things to come when certain sections of the tram network succumbed to buses in

Like most tramway systems, Glasgow ran illuminated cars for special events. In 1957 Permanent Way car No.36 toured the city in connection with a mass X-Ray campaign and is seen here spreading the word in Jamaica Street on the evening of 30th March. The last illuminated tram ran in 1959 for the Scottish Industries Exhibition at Kelvin Hall.

Although standard gauge (4ft 8½in) was stipulated in the Glasgow Tramways Act of 1870, a non-standard gauge was adopted for the whole system because of the relatively minor Vale of Clyde Tramway - surely a case of the tail wagging the dog! The Act of 1871 authorising the Govan line required that provision be made for the passage of railway vehicles and that the gauge must be uniform with the Glasgow tracks. Experiments determined that a gauge of 4ft 7¾in was the most satisfactory, enabling standard gauge locomotives and wagons to run on their flanges in the grooves - where the tramcar wheels ran. On 26th February 1958, a 1924 Andrew Barclay pug uses the tram tracks in Renfrew Road to get from Shieldhall goods depot to the Linthouse shipyard of Alexander Stephen & Sons Ltd. There was a similar arrangement in Govan for the Fairfield yard. The trams ceased in 1958 but rail traffic continued until 1968.

the eventual replacement of trams by buses and trolleybuses. At the time, these proposals must have seemed unthinkable to most of Glasgow's citizens, for the 1,150 'caurs' working 32 routes from eleven depots were surely the lifeblood of the city, despite the buses and trains. But Glasgow was no longer the compact place it used to be when the trams were in their ascendancy; many people had moved from tightly packed tenements to peripheral estates far from the tracks. The British Railways modernisation plan of 1955 endorsed the electrification of local railways and the Corporation was virtually obliged to abandon outlying routes. At the same time they decided to withdraw 450 Standard trams, some of which dated from 1898. Inevitably, these were replaced by buses, over a thousand of which entered service between 1947 and 1958.

Nationally, the tide of opinion had been against trams for some time. They were extinct in the Midlands and south of England, although Liverpool, Leeds, Sheffield and even Edinburgh had held out for a while. When these cities decided to follow the trend, Glasgow's huge system was out on a limb. Therefore, the decision made on 5th February 1958 to abandon the network as soon as possible, and certainly within fifteen years, came as no surprise. *The Glasgow Herald* went along with the mood of the day and stated that 'it will not be popular if trams are still running at the end of 1963'. Elimination of the faithful 'caurs' proceeded faster than even the anti-tram lobby expected and the final farewell took place on 4th September

1948-49. One of these closures was service 2 from Provanmill to Polmadie, which was replaced by the city's first trolleybus route. The use of trolleybuses had been sanctioned way back in 1934, but despite the delay a number of routes were eventually established and the fleet numbered 195 by 1958.

In 1951 the Glasgow and District Transport Committee, under

the chairmanship of Sir Robert Inglis, issued a report addressing transport matters in the Clyde Valley. Congested city centre streets and spare capacity on local railways (two of which passed through the middle of Glasgow in tunnels) claimed particular attention. Inglis recommended the immediate abandonment of outlying tram services, the electrification of local railways, and

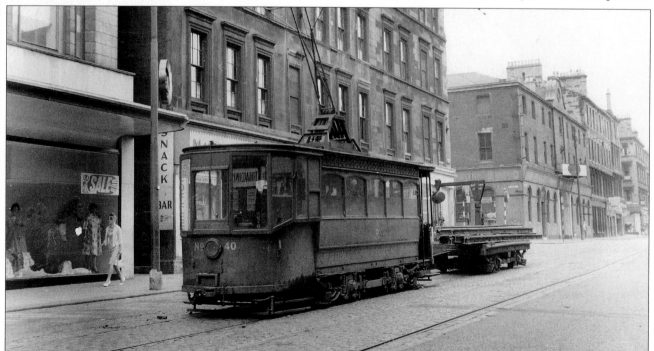

A sad duty for Permanent Way Department vehicles during the closing years of the system was the removal of track on abandoned routes. No.40, converted from a Standard car in 1954, carries out this work near the Sauchiehall Street end of Cambridge Street on 3rd July 1960, following the withdrawal of services 1 and 30 four months previously. On the left, a trendy young lady strides past a fashion shop. This was a hint of the forthcoming 'Swinging Sixties' - an era which seemingly had no place for the trams.

1962. The special procession was watched by a quarter of a million people, despite torrential rain, and a sense of loss prevailed. Could the wrong decision have been made?

For the next three decades, Britain remained tramless apart from the line between Blackpool and Fleetwood along the seafront. Detractors have dismissed this as a holiday resort novelty, conveniently ignoring the fact that it provides efficient transport along an urban corridor throughout the year. Meanwhile, most European cities cherished and improved their tramways. Even the United States remained faithful to urban light railways. Manchester's Metrolink therefore came as a breath of fresh air in a country gradually being choked by motor traffic. The South Yorkshire Supertrams are also a pointer to the future, despite their disappointing start. But what of Glasgow? An east-west tram route through the city centre has recently been proposed, but was rejected on planning grounds. With yet another change in the tide of public opinion, a new version of the 'caurs' will probably appear early in the new Millenium. At least the city has a comprehensive network of electrified

suburban railways, as suggested by Inglis back in 1951, when the trams seemed immortal.

As the system shrank, the number of visiting enthusiasts increased. On 2nd June 1962, two Coronations were required to carry a Light Railway Transport League party over the surviving tracks. During the tour, Nos.1260 and 1269 pause at Scotstoun lye in Balmoral Street, near a bridge carrying the Central Low Level line.

Below. Ordinary tram services finished in Glasgow around midnight on Saturday 1st September 1962. However, a special service operated at a fare of sixpence from Anderston Cross to Auchenshuggle until the evening of Tuesday 4th September, when the farewell procession from Dalmarnock Depot to Coplawhill Works was watched by a quarter of a million people in torrential rain. Indeed, the weather during the dying days of the system was appropriately gloomy, as can be seen in this view of Coronations Nos.1174 and 1243, at Auchenshuggle on 3rd September 1962.

Despite its official funeral, the Glasgow tram was not quite dead as Clydebank had been promised a last tram ceremony of its own. This duly took place on Thursday 6th September 1962. There were gloomy forecasts that the tram would be towed by a breakdown wagon or even brought on a low loader. However, Coronation No.1282 left Dalmarnock Depot under its own power, showing service No.9 and ran through a tramless city on the overcast but dry evening. At the Municipal Buildings in the Burgh of Clydebank it picked up a party of dignitaries watched by a small crowd, mainly children, and departed at 7.14pm for Dalmuir West. The car arrived back at Clydebank half an hour later, then returned to Dalmarnock Depot. No.1282 is now preserved at Crich.

Although there was a rush to rid Glasgow of its cars, the Corporation was more than happy to retain something of its tramway heritage for future generations. On 8th August 1962 a line of restored cars pose outside Coplawhill Works. From front to back they are: round dash Standard No.779 in 1910 condition, hexagaonal dash Standard No.1088 as running in the 1930s, 'Room and Kitchen' single decker No.672 in substantially original condition and horse tram No.543 more or less as built. Together with Coronation No.1173, Cunarder No.1392 and experimental single decker No.1089, they can now be seen in the Museum of Transport at Kelvin Hall.